First published in Great Britain in 1996 by

BROCKHAMPTON PRESS,

20 Bloomsbury Street,

London WC1B 3QA.

a member of the Hodder Headline Group,

This series of little gift books was made by Frances Banfield, Andrea P.A. Belloli, Polly Boyd,
Kate Brown, Stefano Carantini, Laurel Clark, Penny Clarke, Clive Collins, Jack Cooper, Melanie
Cumming, Nick Diggory, John Dunne, Deborah Gill, David Goodman, Paul Gregory, Douglas Hall,
Lucinda Hawksley, Maureen Hill, Dennis Hovell, Dicky Howett, Nick Hutchison, Douglas Ingram,
Helen Johnson, C.M. Lee, Simon London, Irene Lyford, John Maxwell, Patrick McCreeth, Morse
Modaberi, Tara Neill, Sonya Newland, Anne Newman, Grant Oliver, Ian Powling, Terry Price,
Michelle Rogers, Mike Seabrook, Nigel Soper, Karen Sullivan and Nick Wells.

Compilation and selection copyright © 1996 Brockhampton Press.

ISBN 1 86019 432X

A copy of the CIP data is available from the British Library upon request.

Produced for Brockhampton Press by Flame Tree Publishing,
a part of The Foundry Creative Media Company Limited,
The Long House, Antrobus Road, Chiswick W4 5HY.

Printed and bound in Italy by L.E.G.O. Spa.

THE LITTLE BOOK
OF
Victoriana

Selected by Karen Sullivan

BROCKHAMPTON PRESS

Men never think, at least seldom think, what a hard
task it is for us women to go through this very often.
God's will be done, and if He decrees that we are to
have a great number of children why we must try to
bring them up as useful and exemplary
members of society.

Queen Victoria

When the Golden Sun is sinking
And your mind from care is free
When you are thinking of your friends
Won't you sometimes think of me?

Victorian valentine

We women are not made for governing — and if we are
good women, we must dislike these masculine
occupations; but there are times which force one to
take interest in them mal gré —
bon gré, and I do, of course, intensely.

Queen Victoria

They're subjects of Queen Victoria, asuch and be
thankful to have a decent Government over 'em.

Flora Thompson, *Lark Rise to Candleford*

Knew her own mind. But the mind radically
commonplace, only its inherited force, & cumulative
sense of power, making it remarkable.

Virginia Woolf, Diary entry on Queen Victoria, 27 December 1930

What's the use? She would only want me to
take a message to dear Albert.

Benjamin Disraeli, attributed last words on hearing that Queen
Victoria wanted to see him

See-saw, Margery Daw,
Jacky shall have a new master,
Jacky shall have but a penny a day,
Because he can't work any faster.

Victorian nursery rhyme

ENGINE BRAND

IMPREGNATED   IMPREGNATED

SAFETY MATCHES
MADE IN SWEDEN

THE
MOTOR GIRL

SAFETY MATCH
MADE IN SWEDEN

A fare admirer.

WILLS'S CIGARETTES.

46

GIVE LIGHT

ENGLAND'S

MORELAND

TRADE   MARK

GLOUCESTER

MADE   GOODS

GLORY

❧ 9 ❧

The people, in their Sunday best, were streaming
towards the lychgate of the church. The squire and the
farmers wore top hats, and the squire's head gardener
and the schoolmaster and the village carpenter.
The farm labourers wore bowlers or,
the older men, soft, round black felts.

Flora Thompson, *Lark Rise to Candleford*

The higher the mountain
The cooler the breeze
The younger the couple
The tighter the squeeze

Victorian rhyme

In summer the carriage was at the door at three o'clock
in the afternoon to take the lady of the house and her
grown-up daughters, if any, to pay calls. If they found
no one in, they left cards, turned down at the corner, or
not turned down, according to etiquette.

Flora Thompson, *Lark Rise to Candleford*

A Happy Christmas

Who is Mary Mitford but the perfect Victorian Englishwoman; her books, her records, her transcriptions bring alive an age that brings alive its Queen. She is the rural Dickens, she draws the classic evocation of Victorian country life. Her garden is that famous little Victorian paradise.

...she is herself better and stronger than any of her books; and her letters and conversation show more grasp of intellect and general power than would be inferable from her finished compositions...In her works, however, through all the beauty there is a clear vein of sense, and a quickness of observation which takes the character of a refined shrewdness...And is she not besides most intensely a woman, and an Englishwoman?

Elizabeth Barrett Browning on Mary Russell Mitford

'For oh,' say the children, 'we are weary,
And we cannot run or leap;
If we cared for any meadows, it were merely
To drop down in them and sleep.
Our knees tremble sorely in the stooping,
We fall upon our faces, trying to go;
And, underneath our heavy eyelids drooping,
The reddest flower would look as pale as snow;
For, all day, we drag our burden tiring
Through the coal-dark, underground -
Or, all day, we drive the wheels of iron
In the factories, round and round.'

Elizabeth Barrett Browning, 'The Cry of the Children'

The Queen is most anxious to enlist everyone who can
speak or write to join in checking this mad, wicked folly
of 'Woman's Rights' with all its attendant horrors on
which her poor, feeble sex is bent, forgetting every
sense of womanly feeling and propriety.

Queen Victoria to Sir Theodore Martin

Two in a car
Two little kisses
Two weeks later
Mr and Mrs

Victorian rhyme

In the year of Queen Victoria's Golden Jubilee,
in 1887, jam could be bought in glass jars inscribed
'1837 to 1887. Victoria the Good,' and underneath,
'Peace and Plenty'.

If I'm in heaven and you're not there
I'll carve your name on the golden chair
For all the angels there to see
I love you and you love me.
And if you're not there by judgement day
I'll know you've gone the other way
So just to prove my love is true
I'll go to hell just to be with you.

Victorian rhyme

A Posy for Mother.

"A POSY for
          Mother,
        because
she's kind,
The sweetest
  flowers that
    I could
      find!"

"What do you
    want for them?"
        Mother said,
Tenderly patting
    the curly head.

"Twenty kisses,"
    said Baby May—
"Dreadful ex-
    pensive flowers
        are they!"

But Mother
    bought them,
      because, you know,
They meant:
    "Dear Mother,
        I love you so!"
          C. B.

Jan. 23, 1897.   Short Story, "HUGH MORRISTON," page 173.   Price 1d.

THE YOUNG LADIES' JOURNAL

PATTERN OF SKIRT GRATIS ON RECEIPT OF COUPON
AND STAMPED ADDRESSED WRAPPER.

"NO FRIEND LIKE AN OLD FRIEND."

No. 1,712.   London: HARRISON & VILES, Merton House, Salisbury Square, Fleet Street, E.C.   THE YOUNG LADIES' JOURNAL
PAPER PATTERN COUPON, No. 1,712.

His purity was too great, his aspiration too high for this
poor, miserable world! His great soul is now only
enjoying that for which it was worthy!

Queen Victoria at the death of Prince Albert

Here come three tinkers, three by three,
To court your daughter, fair lady,
Oh, can we have a lodging here, here, here?
Oh, can we have a lodging here?

Victorian children's game

I don't dislike babies, though I think very young ones
rather disgusting.

Queen Victoria

Step and fetch her, step and fetch her,
Step and fetch her, pretty little dear.
Do not tease her, try and please her,
Step and fetch her, pretty little dear.

Victorian dancing song

Travelling tinkers with their barrows, braziers, and
twirling grindstones turned aside from the main road
and came singing:

Any razors or scissors to grind?

Or anything else in the tinker's line?

Any old pots or kettles to mend?

Flora Thompson, *Lark Rise to Candleford*

God made trees,
Man made fences,
God made the boys,
To kiss pretty wenches.

Victorian rhyme

Here is a stall glittering with new tin saucepans; there another, bright with its blue and yellow crockery, and sparkling with white glass.

Henry Mayhew, *Mayhew's London*

The pastry and confectionery which tempt the street eaters are tarts of rhubarb, currant, gooseberry, cherry, apple, damson, cranberry, and mince pies; plum dough and plum-cake, lard, currant, almond and many other varieties of cakes, as well as of tarts; gingerbread-nuts and heart-cakes; Chelsea buns; muffins and crumpets; lozenges, candies, and hard-bakes.

Henry Mayhew, *Mayhew's London*

And what should they know of England who only
England know?

Rudyard Kipling

Her court was pure; her life serene;
God gave her peace; her land reposed;
A thousand claims to reverence closed
In her a Mother, Wife and Queen.

Alfred, Lord Tennyson, 'To the Queen'

It is a far, far better thing that I do, than I have ever
done; it is a far, far better rest that I go to, than I have
ever known.

Charles Dickens, *A Tale of Two Cities*

Wee Willie Winkie runs through the town,
Upstairs and downstairs in his nightgown,
Rapping at the window, crying through the lock,
Are the children all in bed, for now it's eight o'clock.

Victorian nursery rhyme

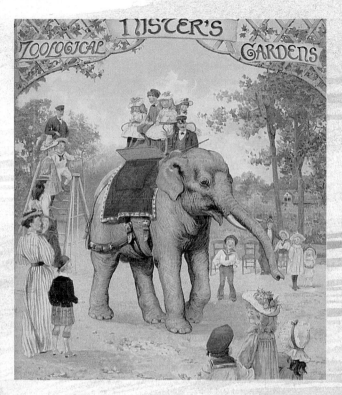

Oh yet we trust that somehow good
Will be the final goal of ill!

Alfred, Lord Tennyson

To be in it [Society] is merely a bore.
But to be out of it is simply a tragedy.

Oscar Wilde, *A Woman of No Importance*

Withers: They have named another battleship after
Queen Victoria, Madam.
Lady D: Another? She must be beginning to think there
is some resemblance.

Alan Bennett, *Forty Years On*

When you've shouted Rule Britannia, when you've
sung God Save the Queen,
When you've finished killing Kruger with your
mouth...

Rudyard Kipling, *The Absent-Minded Beggar*

This is a London particular... A fog, miss.

Charles Dickens, *Bleak House*

When my mother died I was very young.
And my father sold me while yet my tongue
Could scarcely cry, 'weep! weep! weep!'
So your chimneys I sweep, and in soot I sleep.

William Blake, 'The Chimney Sweeper'

Your Majesty is the head of the Literary profession.

Benjamin Disraeli to Queen Victoria

Lord Darlington: Nowadays, we are all of us so poor,
the only things we can pay are compliments.

Oscar Wilde, *Lady Windermere's Fan*

The United Metropolitan Improved Hot Muffin and
Crumpet Baking and Punctual Delivery Company.

Charles Dickens, *Nicholas Nickleby*

The omnibus conductor, who is vulgarly known as the
'cad', stands on a small projection at the end of the
omnibus; and it is his office to admit and set down
every passenger, and to receive the amount of fare.
He is paid four shillings a day,
which he is allowed to stop out of the
monies he receives.

Henry Mayhew, *Mayhew's London*

If you were a postcard
And I the stamp could be
I'd lick you till I'm sure you stick
Through thick and thin to me.

Victorian valentine

What a pity it is that we have no amusements in
England but vice and religion!

Sydney Smith

He speaks to Me as if I was a public meeting.

Queen Victoria about Prime Minister W. E. Gladstone

Take of English earth as much
As either hand may rightly clutch.
In the taking of it breathe
Prayer for all who lie beneath.

Rudyard Kipling, 'A Charm'

PANTOMIME

A

WOOD AND **ARTHUR COLLINS.**

And statesmen at her council met
Who knew the seasons when to take
Occasion by the hand and make
The bounds of freedom wider yet.

Alfred, Lord Tennyson, 'To the Queen'

In the parlour there were three
She, the parlour lamp and he
Two is company, three is a crowd
And so the parlour lamp went out.

Victorian rhyme

The principal sale of milk from the cow is in St James's
Park. There are eight stands in the summer, and as
many cows: but in the winter there are only four cows.

Henry Mayhew, *Mayhew's London*

We've got a private master comes to teach us at home,
but we ain't proud, because ma says it's sinful.

Charles Dickens, *Nicholas Nickleby*

Children's nursery hours should be as follows: All out of bed at seven, all dressed and sitting down to breakfast at eight, nine o'clock should see the little troop out of doors in garden, in park, or on country roads. Two hours' walk in the morning and two in the afternoon is necessary in fine weather. After the 20th of October all children under six should be indoors after three o'clock: this rule should be continued until spring days again come round.

Mrs Beeton's Every Day Cookery and Housekeeping Book

A pretty, graceful game to watch was 'Thread the Tailor's Needle'. For this two girls joined both hands and elevated them to form an arch or bridge, and the other players, in single file and holding on to each other's skirts, passed under, singing:

Thread the Tailor's needle,
Thread the Tailor's needle,
The tailor's blind and he can't see,
So thread the tailor's needle.

Flora Thompson, *Lark Rise to Candleford*

'Pin-a sights' were flower petal arrangements pressed between two small sheets of glass and covered by a brown paper flap.

A pin to see a pin-a-sight,
All the ladies dressed in white.
A pin behind and a pin before,
And a pin to knock at the lady's door.

Flora Thompson, *Lark Rise to Candleford*

It is thought that Prince Albert, Queen Victoria's husband, introduced the custom of the Christmas tree from his native Germany. The trees were lit by wax candles and decorated with small gifts.

The rich man in his castle,
The poor man at his gate,
God made them, high or lowly,
And ordered their estate.

Hymn by Mrs C. F. Alexander

The Sketch

1898

Christmas Number

Dead! and never called me mother!

Mrs Henry Wood, *East Lynne*

Worry not over the future,
The present is all thou hast,
The future will soon be the present,
And the present will soon be the past.

Victorian rhyme

I remember, I remember,
The home where I was born,
The little window where the sun
Came peeping in at morn ...

Thomas Hood, 'I Remember, I Remember'

There is too much of it. I do not like sightseeing
anyway. This was too many sights in one place!

Charles Dickens on his visit to the Great Exhibition

This is one of the greatest and most glorious days of our lives. Upon the Crystal Palace the flags of every nation were flying. This peace festival is uniting the industry and art of all nations of the earth. It was a day to live forever.

Queen Victoria, Diary entry on the day she opened the Great Exhibition, 1 May 1851

It's hard when folk can find no work
Where they've been bred and born.
When I was young I always thought
I'd grind my bread from corn.
But I've been forced to work in town
So here's my Litany:
'From Hull and Halifax and Hell
Good Lord, deliver me.'

'The Dalesman's Litany'

For many miles before they reached it they saw
a grey cloud hanging over the town. They
crossed the long, straight, hopeless streets of
houses, all the same, all small. They had to stop
constantly for wagons. Margaret had visited
London, there had been several sorts of traffic
there. Here every vehicle carried
goods to do with cotton.

Elizabeth Gaskell, *North and South*

Polly put the kettle on,
Polly put the kettle on,
Polly put the kettle on,
    We'll all have tea.
Sukey take it off again,
Sukey take it off again,
Sukey take it off again,
    They've all gone away.

Quoted by Charles Dickens in *Barnaby Rudge*

Here we go round the mulberry bush,
The mulberry bush, the mulberry bush,
Here we go round the mulberry bush,
On a cold and frosty morning.

This is the way we clap our hands,
Clap our hands, clap our hands,
This is the way we clap our hands,
On a cold and frosty morning.

Victorian nursery rhyme

Ring-a-ring o'roses,
A pocket full of posies,
A-tishoo! A-tishoo!
We all fall down.

Kate Greenaway, *Mother Goose*

Early to bed and early to rise
Makes a man healthy, wealthy, and wise.

Victorian proverb

The Queen of Hearts
She made some tarts,
All on a summer's day;
The Knave of Hearts
He stole the tarts,
And took them clean away.

Lewis Carroll, *Alice's Adventures in Wonderland*

Now, what I want is, Facts. Teach these boys and girls
nothing but Facts. Facts alone are wanted in life. Plant
nothing else, and root out everything else.

Charles Dickens, *Hard Times*

Little Polly Flinders
Sat among the cinders,
Warming her pretty little toes;
Her mother came and caught her,
And whipped her little daughter
For spoiling her nice new clothes.

John Harris, Victorian nursery rhyme

A Victorian Mayonnaise

2 egg yolks
half pint of olive oil
1 tablespoon plain or tarragon vinegar
veal jelly
pinch of salt
pinch of cayenne pepper
1 clove garlic
capers

Put in a large basin the yolks only of two large fresh eggs with salt and cayenne pepper. Stir, then add one teaspoon of the best salad oil and work mixture until it appears like a cream. Pour in by slow degrees nearly half a pint of oil, until the sauce has the smoothness of a custard and no oil remains visible. Then add a tablespoon of plain or tarragon vinegar and one tablespoon of cold water to whiten the sauce. A lump of clear veal jelly the size of an egg much improves it, and a morsel of garlic not larger than a pea. A few French capers may be added.

Solomon Grundy,
Born on Monday,
Christened on Tuesday,
Married on Wednesday,
Took ill on Thursday,
Worse on Friday,
Died on Saturday,
Buried on Sunday,
This is the end
Of Solomon Grundy.

Rhyme used in Victorian England
to teach children the days of the week

Under the spreading chestnut tree
The village smithy stands;
The smith, a mighty man is he,
With large and sinewy hands;
And the muscles of his brawny arms
Are strong as iron bands.

Henry Wadsworth Longfellow, 'The Village Blacksmith'

Lady – ought to get a good whipping. It is a subject which makes the Queen so furious that she cannot contain herself. God created men and women different – then let them remain each in their own position.

Queen Victoria to Sir Theodore Martin

I mourn the safe and motherly old middle-class queen, who held the nation warm under the fold of her big, hideous Scotch-plaid shawl and whose duration had been so extraordinarily convenient and beneficent. I felt her death much more than I should have expected; she was a sustaining symbol – and the wild waters are upon us now.

Henry James

Hullo! Father Christmas
Are you there?
ERNEST NISTER. LONDON
E. P. DUTTON & Co NEW YORK

EDUCATION – At Mr Wackford Squeer's Academy,
Dotheboys Hall, at the delightful village of Dotheboys,
near Greta Bridge in Yorkshire, Youth are boarded,
clothed, booked, furnished with pocket-money,
provided with all necessaries, instructed in all
languages living and dead, mathematics, orthography,
geometry, astronomy, trigonometry, the use of the
globes, algebra, single stick (if required), writing,
arithmetic, fortification, and every other branch of
classical literature. Terms, twenty guineas per annum.
No extras. No vacations, and diet unparalleled.

Charles Dickens, *Nicholas Nickleby*

The poor fatherless baby of eight months is now
the utterly broken-hearted and crushed widow of
forty-two! My life as a happy one is ended! The
world is gone for me! If I must live on (and I will
do nothing to make me worse than I am), it is
henceforth for our poor fatherless children —
for my unhappy country, which has lost all in
losing him — and in only doing what I know
and feel he would wish.

Queen Victoria, Letter to King Leopold of the Belgians on
Prince Albert's death, 1861

Land of our birth, we pledge to thee
Our love and toil in the years to be;
When we are grown and take our place,
As men and women with our race.

Rudyard Kipling

We are not amused.

Queen Victoria

If!

If to be wishful
still to linger
near thee

If when thy
name be
spoken

Skittles is a favourite amusement, and the
costermongers class themselves among the best players
in London. The game is always for beer,
but betting goes on.

Henry Mayhew, *Mayhew's London*

Kiss under a lily
Kiss under a rose
But the best place to kiss
Is under the nose

Victorian valentine

Somewhere the sun is shining,
Somewhere a little rain,
Somewhere a heart is pining
For love, but all in vain;
Somewhere a soul is drifting
Further and far apart,
Somewhere my love is dreaming,
Somewhere a broken heart.

Victorian song

I positively think that ladies who are always enceinte
are quite disgusting; it is more like a rabbit or guinea-
pig than anything else and really it is not very nice.

Queen Victoria

'Twas about the time of Christmas, and many years ago,
When the sky was black with wrath and rack,
and the earth was white with snow...
Hemmed in by hungry billows,
whose madness foamed at lip,
Half a mile from the shore,
or hardly more, she saw a gallant ship...

Jane Conquest, a Victorian melodrama

Curly locks, Curly locks,
Wilt thou be mine?
Thou shalt not wash dishes
Nor yet feed the swine;
But sit on a cushion
And sew a fine seam,
And feed upon strawberries,
Sugar and cream.

Victorian nursery rhyme

NOTES ON ILLUSTRATIONS

Page 6 *The Sketch Xmas Number 1895.* Courtesy of the Laurel Clark Collection; **Page 9** *Three Matchbox Labels and a Cigarette Card* (Private Collection). Courtesy of The Bridgeman Art Library; **Page 11** *Two Girls With Mistletoe.* Courtesy of The Laurel Clark Collection; **Pages 12-13** *Scene at a Victorian Circus, c.1872* (Victoria and Albert Museum, London). Courtesy of The Bridgeman Art Library; **Page 15** *Souvenir Programme of the Opening of Tower Bridge, June 30th 1894* (Private Collection). Courtesy of The Bridgeman Art Library; **Page 17** *Punch, Judy, Baby and Dog.* Courtesy of the Laurel Clark Collection; **Page 19** *A Posy for Mother.* Courtesy of The Laurel Clark Collection; **Page 20** *Young Ladies Journal.* Courtesy of The Laurel Clark Collection; **Page 22** *Happy Family Playing Cards, Scaps and Calender, Mid-Victorian* (Private Collection). Courtesy of The Bridgeman Art Library; **Page 25** *Zoological Gardens.* Courtesy of The Laurel Clark Collection; **Page 26-7** *The Royal Children in the Nursery* (Stapleton Collection). Courtesy of The Bridgeman Art Library; **Page 29** *Collection of Victorian Music Hall Programmes, Valentines and Christmas Cards* (John Hall Antiques, London). Courtesy of The Bridgeman Art Library; **Page 32-3** *Poster for 'Cinderella'* by Tom Browne (R. Mander and J. Mitchenson Theatre Coll., Lo). Courtesy of The Bridgeman Art Library; **Page 36** *Playing in the Snow.* Courtesy of The Laurel Clark Collection; **Page 38** *The Sketch Christmas Number, 1898.* Courtesy of The Laurel Clark Collection; **Page 41** *The Gentlewoman's Record of the Glorious Reign of Victoria the Good.* Courtesy of The Laurel Clark Collection; **Page 42** *Punch in Action.* Courtesy of The Laurel Clark Collection; **Page 44** *Buttercup Pictures.* Courtesy of The Laurel Clark Collection; **Page 47** *Pears - Matchless for the Complexion.* Courtesy of The Laurel Clark Collection; **Page 48** *Christmas Number London Opinion.* Courtesy of The Laurel Clark Collection; **Page 51** *Mother Goose Jingles.* Courtesy of The Laurel Clark Collection; **Pages 52-3** *Calender from 'The Queen', 1887 with Portraits of Queen Victoria and Prince Albert* (Private Collection). Courtesy of The Bridgeman Art Library; **Page 55** *Hullo! Father Christmas.* Courtesy of The Laurel Clark Collection; **Page 56** *Queen Anne pack of playing cards, depicting the Queen, the Marlboroughs and various victorious battles of the Marlboroughs* (Blenheim Palace, Oxfordshire). Courtesy of The Bridgeman Art Library; **Page 58** *Victorian Scented Greetings Card* (Private Collection). Courtesy of The Bridgeman Art Library.

Acknowledgements: The Publishers wish to thank everyone who gave permission to reproduce the quotes in this book. Every effort has been made to contact the copyright holders, but in the event that an oversight has occurred, the publishers would be delighted to rectify any omissions in future editions of this book. Letters of Virginia Woolf, copyright © the Estate of Virginia Woolf; Rudyard Kipling reprinted courtesy of Macmillan Publishing Company Limited.